In the Beginning

An Osprey Family Story

by Elliott Carr

Foreword

By Wayne R. Petersen

Director, Massachusetts Audubon Important Bird Areas Program

For eons birds have had special relevance to humans. To our early ancestors birds represented sustenance and later they were hunted for sport. Today the childhood memory of a baby bird rescued from the clutches of a cat and ultimately triaged into a flying adult, or the haunting nocturnal wailing of loons at a remote lakeshore near a beloved summer retreat are events that remain with us forever. For folks living within the sight and sound of Ospreys, however, it is the piercing early spring courtship calls and the spectacular aerial plunges of the indomitable "Fish Hawk" which evoke memories that are unforgettable.

Nearly cosmopolitan in distribution, the Osprey *(Pandion haliaetus)* is potentially found wherever extensive water bodies exist. Feeding almost completely on fish, their dynamic foraging strategy offers a constant source of admiration and entertainment for anyone privileged to watch. Adaptable and remarkably trusting of humans, Ospreys have learned to live within ready proximity to people, often building their large and conspicuous nests on everything from cell towers and power line stanchions to navigation buoys and platforms specifically constructed for their use. Where they are common, they assume rock star status – beloved and admired by all who come in contact with them.

In Massachusetts the Osprey population stood at fewer than a dozen pairs in the 1960s. During the mid-20th century Ospreys, along with Brown Pelicans, Bald Eagles, Peregrine Falcons, and various other predatory birds high on the food chain were severely impacted by eating fish contaminated with long-lasting, polychlorinated hydrocarbon pesticides such as DDT. The resultant affect of eggshell thinning nearly caused the demise of successful breeding populations of these species throughout the northeastern United States. With thanks in large measure to Rachel Carson and her prescient opus, *Silent Spring* (1962), DDT and several other hard pesticides were banned in 1972, thus beginning an era of recovery for beleaguered northeastern Osprey populations. Today the Bay State hosts close to 200 pairs.

Though much has been written about this iconic species, few authors have photographically captured this species with the intimacy exhibited by Elliott Carr. Spending hours patiently observing a local pair of Ospreys, the author eventually came to know Adam and Eve (as he affectionately called them) as individuals, thoughtfully interpreting their vocal utterances and tracking their every move with photographic precision. The result is a unique, sensitive, and complete visual record that captures seemingly every nuance of a pair of Ospreys living on the shore of Cape Cod Bay. Carr's artful accounting of the life of breeding Ospreys is exhaustively complete, despite the inevitable void created in the life history of this species when it departs Cape Cod for the winter. Fortunately, we have an increasingly complete body of knowledge built on the results of satellite tracking of Ospreys that helps fill the gaps in the life history of these long-distance Neotropical migrants once they leave the United States for the winter.

The combination of Carr's stunning and often intimate photography combined with appropriately sensitive vignettes about the domestic life of Ospreys make this book an aesthetically valuable contribution to our understanding of this iconic raptor.

1. Unholy Matrimony

Ospreys live on every continent except Antarctica, their lives unchanged by the passage of time except for coping with the havoc wrought by man.

Each spring two osprey punctually return around April 1 to their nest high above a salt marsh in Brewster MA where Paines Creek winds past Wings Island between the mainland and the widest sand flats in North America.

West Brewster serves as my Garden of Eden: a place to observe natural events as aptly-named Stony Brook flows from three tranquil mill ponds over 22 small waterfalls, pierces a small patch of near total wilderness, then crosses the marsh past Wings Island with the name Paines Creek reflecting its renewed tranquility, and finally migrates through ever-shifting low-tide channels across the flats into Cape Cod Bay.

Under osprey common law, pairs mate for life. But like humans, they cope with death, divorce, and occasional affairs.

I call the Paines Creek osprey Eve and Adam, and enjoy sitting many mornings and evenings behind my tripod photographing them. I always wear the same blue clothes to make sure Eve and Adam recognize my species. Osprey live without government, religion or cash as a means to exchange material goods. Their life evolves around the food chain: which species eats which others to stay alive.

Adam and Eve have welcomed me like part of their family.

I'm not a naturalist and don't maintain a lifetime bird list. But I hope to compile the best-ever osprey family photograph album as a means of better understanding another species. I know I won't, but it's important to have goals.

I enjoy observing osprey more than humans. They're more overt, don't try to cover up their bad habits however cruel to the fish they eat, and the routine of their lives make everyone more equal.

Male osprey with happy memories of successful
nests return north first each spring to reclaim
their nests before some other male stakes a
claim. Some years, arrival is followed by a
week or more of turmoil over repossession,
or reestablishment, or severance of
partnerships. Adam returns in a clean
new suit. He tidies up the nest waiting
for Eve (or another partner), then
seduces her to start another family.
They frolic overhead until eggs
tie Eve to the nest.

Osprey are cold-blooded Machiavellians when it comes to family matters. Males seek a partner capable of raising two or three young a year. Females select capable providers, evaluating male ability to procure fish to eat and sticks for their nest; each year they make males reprove themselves for a few days before partnering. Sometimes a match doesn't work; the osprey separate or divorce.

6

Female and male osprey look somewhat alike. But females weigh approximately 15% more than males. Long-legged males, who spend their summers flying and high diving for fish, often appear slimmer, whiter and fitter. Male osprey stand taller.

Both male and female osprey have dark brown wing tops over white bottoms which blend with the ground when viewed from above, and with the sky from below.

Compared to males, female osprey in summer look like couch potatoes who don't get as much exercise. Plumper, most females wear what many birders label necklaces. But they more resemble a bib.

11

Female osprey chest feathers also serve as a
camouflaged layer of insulation and protection
on the front windward wall of the nest chamber
in which female osprey protect their eggs –
and young – from cold, wind, rain; occasionally
even sleet or snow.

12

Absence makes osprey hearts grow fonder as they return north. April differs dramatically from the remainder of the summer, with Eve and Adam's roles sometimes reversed.

13

Adam leaps on Eve several times a day to copulate, sometimes with grass on his feet or even while she is eating.

14

Eve, crushed on the nest, responds with variable enthusiasm, lifting her tail to the side when willing to provide access. Not long after eggs arrive, Adam's interest diminishes, as if nature turned off a switch.

15

2008

How many years have the same Eve and Adam occupied the Brewster nest?

It's romantic to think osprey mate for life. But how long do they really, and how long do they live?

Eve and Adam change in appearance every year, particularly Eve's necklace/ bib/ chest insulation. Eve dons a new necklace and Adam a new t-shirt; in biological terms both molt new feathers. Eve comes north sometimes with darker feathers spotted below her waist.

2009

2010

Eve and Adam's behavior also changes every year, in some years more noticeably than others. The 2011 osprey looked and behaved entirely differently from their predecessors.

Maybe they just get older or it's the weather or other osprey or as with man a particularly good or bad fishing year. In 2011 both seemed far more wary of other osprey and large birds, as if they were young learning their role.

Lacking DNA tests, I suspect there may have been 2 or 3 Eves and the same number of Adams over the past 7 years.

2011

2. The Food Chain

Eve and Adam return at the same time sea herring (alewife) scouts begin running up Paines Creek to spawn in its headwater ponds.

In 1767, herring trapped near 22 small waterfalls upstream became the initial raw material at historic Factory Village, one of Cape Cod's first industrial sites, fueled by waterpower from the falls. The same natural abundance had attracted Saquatucket Indians and osprey thousands of years before, as well as John Wing, Brewster's first recorded white settler, in 1657.

Overfishing all but eliminated the run and osprey disappeared from Cape Cod by 1962 when Rachel Carson hypothesized in **Silent Spring** that the chemical DDT, ingested through fish, destroyed the shells of unborn birds. Carson was vilified by chemical manufacturers and the U.S. Dept. of Agriculture for making such assertions in a controversy reminiscent of that concerning global warming today. But after Carson's death, an investigation by President Kennedy's Scientific Advisory Committee vindicated her work. In 1972 sale of DDT was banned.

Massachusetts Audubon now monitors approximately 200 osprey nests, including Eve and Adam's on the salt marsh behind the Cape Cod Museum of Natural History.

"A river herring's lot in life is to be eaten," Philip Oates, retired Director of the Massachusetts Division of Marine Fisheries opined at a conference in Brewster a few years ago. Herring served pickled and salted played a major role in the early days of Cape Cod as a staple of colonial diets, bait, and fertilizer. Brewster's catch was "extraordinary," historian Joseph Paine noted; colonists once took over 200 barrels in a single day before running out of both salt and barrels. Alewives played such a strong role in the Cape economy and diet that the fishery became its first regulated industry, before the town bought the run in 1786.

Alewives enroute to spawn have always been very easy to catch as they stop to rest below waterfalls. They can be scooped in buckets or nets and eaten by practically every creature Cape Codders hold dear: striped bass, tuna, seals, and whales, as well as osprey and particularly herring gulls, named after the fish. Alewives spawn like sex-crazed Mayflies. A female lays 60,000 to 250,000 eggs at a time. Only 1% survive summer youth to make the reverse trip back down the run to life at sea. The others get eaten out of growing up.

Licensed fishing companies from as far away as New Bedford parked tank trucks before dawn at the Brewster run to pump live alewives into the tanks before 'harvesting' was banned a few years ago.

Herring runs provide one of nature's bloodiest displays of the role of differing species in the food chain. One can't watch without pondering the meaning of life and the complex, fatalistic, one-sided relationships between species. But birds, fish and animals kill to eat, not for profit or sport. I've never seen an osprey or herring gull fail to devour every small piece of slain alewives.

The Brewster run still seems saturated with alewives circling in shallow pools preparatory to swimming up the next waterfall. Approximately six inches high and one foot long but only one inch wide, they knife up through the cascading water, minimizing loss of speed. Their strong fins provide near instant acceleration to approximately 40 MPH. The climb up each waterfall is only a few feet, each ascension done in the flash of an eye. Alewives know the shortest route starts as close to the underlying stones as possible and exits through the bottom of the deluge above: a quick swim of only 3 to 5 feet.

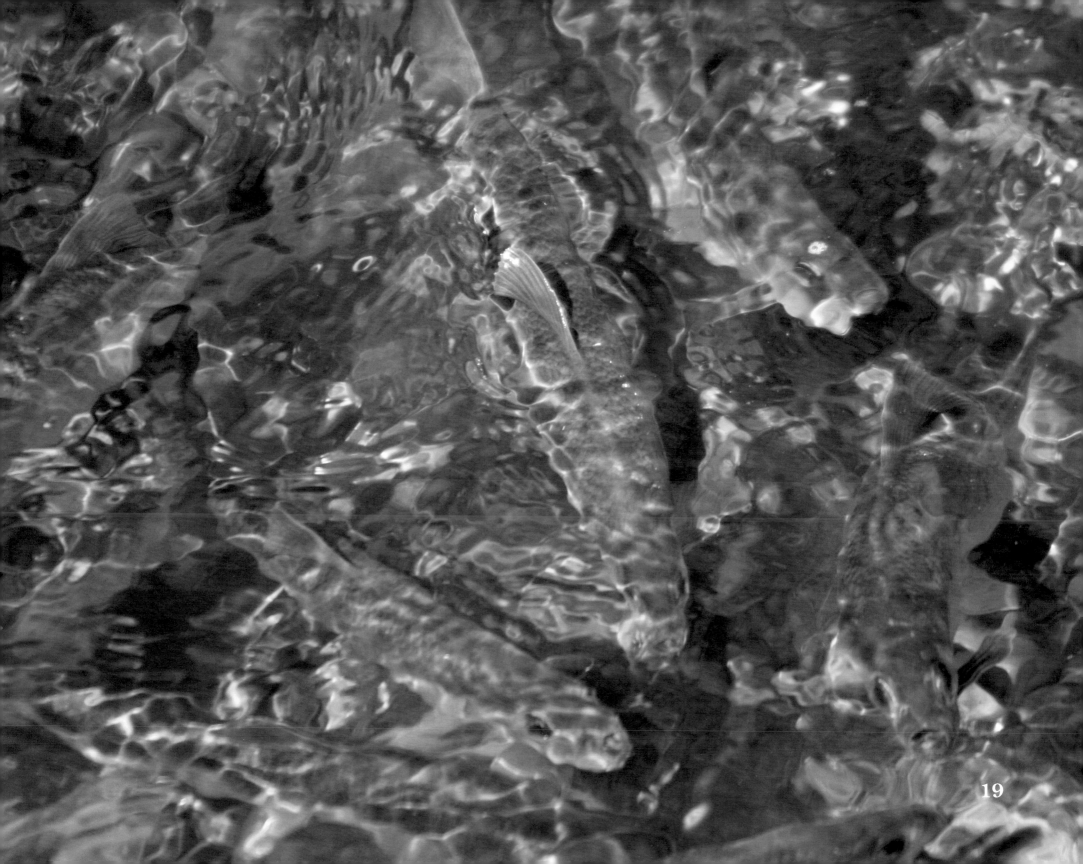

19

Osprey and herring gulls catch and consume their prey differently, contrasting carefully planned precision with near total chaos. Osprey soar almost motionlessly up to 100' above stream, peering intently down positioning their 'dives.'

Osprey's unbending legs and scaled rather than feathered talons and feet are unique among birds, probably leftover from reptile history.

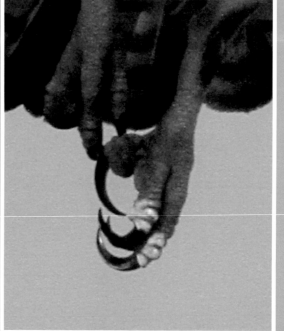

On a successful dive as Adam hits water, four talons at the end of each leg pierce the fish faster than man can blink an eye. The outer talon on each foot pivots in any direction, facilitating simultaneous ice tong like piercing from multiple directions.

21

I always assumed osprey dove down into (and through) the water in a torpedo-like position, maximizing speed and efficiency. But Adam utilizes gravity, free-falling straight down to the water like a young boy dropped feet first from the bottom hatch of an airplane, reaching speeds up to 50 MPH. He extends his tail downward to brake forward momentum, his wings upward to minimize air resistance, while utilizing both wings and tail to make minor course adjustments. His legs and talons extend straight downward to grasp the fish instantaneously upon impact.

If the fish moves too far, Adam aborts his dive mid-flight, flying forward again as abruptly as he started down.

22

Osprey, in contrast to herring gulls, have a short sharply hooked upper beak which they utilize in accompaniment with their talons to grasp a fish firmly then tear it into bite-size pieces. Minute spikes on the beak enable them to hang onto food even when the beak points downward.

24

An osprey's blunt v-shaped lower beak serves as an anvil and contains a channel for food to pass to the stomach. Osprey eat every piece of fish except the intestines, including scales, bone, and fins — except when passing them on to their offspring.

25

Herring gulls, in dramatic contrast to osprey, line the stream banks in great numbers where the brook bubbles over rocks, backing up alewives below each waterfall. Herring gulls seem one of nature's most overtly cruel creatures. Whatever one gull does, others do, not always seeming to recognize other members of their own species.

The gulls peer intently into shallow water, flapping their wings, squawking and trying to poke each other off the best vantage points, poised to leap in to grasp an unfortunate herring.

Their bodies resemble air force cargo planes with torsos large enough to hold an entire fish (or two or three) and gaping mouths resembling the hatches through which tanks and hearses roll onto and off planes.

Gulls prefer to grasp a fish headfirst, then swallow it in a gulp or two, preferably one if other gulls are in position for a tug-of war. If a gull catches a fish sideways, it may drop it on shore to line it up. Occasionally a lucky fish bounces back into the stream.

Three Mouths, One Fish

26

A neighbor and I once watched a gull leap in and out of the water eight times, before securing a 12" herring, half as long as the bird. Its beak darted quickly below water to grasp the fish, as others tried to muscle it away. But it swallowed the fish in a few gulps. It strode around a few minutes with its much enlarged neck and throat pulsating as the still-alive fish thrashed around in the hatch. The faster a gull swallows a fish, the more pronounced the neck pulses.

Our gull made five more jumps to secure its second herring then took considerably more swallows cramming that unfortunate fish into its occupied food locker. Then it tottered of to some nearby rock (or roof) to digest and poop.

3. Upscale High-Rise Home

Osprey once built their homes in trees, ideally with a water view 10' to 60' above the ground. But humans facilitated the specie's rebirth by erecting tall poles with platforms to nest on. Why should a pair of osprey undertake the intensive and time-consuming task of building a 4' by 6' horizontal base holding several hundred pounds of limbs on a tree fork, when man provides platforms for them? Today osprey nest on utility poles, chimneys, roofs, steeples, bridges, cell towers, and other manmade structures, preferring those with cross support. NSTAR, a local power company, erected numerous towers on Cape Cod specifically for osprey nests, hoping to keep the birds off high tension lines — and envisioning favorable public relations. The inset shows the nest in early spring after man has stripped it down; by early summer Eve and Adam have built it back up.

28

Eve and Adam set to work each year air-lifting in tree limbs, leaves, pinecones, seaweed, grass and mud; as well as abandoned fishnets, plastic fences, boards, abandoned clothes, blankets and towels, and whatever other human residue might be around to brighten up and enhance their bathtub-size homes. Tree limbs provide a strong frame and 'ramparts' around the nest edge to restrain chicks from falling out and cut the wind.

Dead grass, seaweed, and mud soften the nest-bed, providing insulation to maintain Eve's warmth for eggs and newly born chicks.

31

Osprey seem fascinated by bright colors; indeed by anything human.

In 2007 Adam flew home carrying a large piece of dead seagull skeleton with a section of skin and feathers attached.

In 2010 he brought back a large bag of trash. A few minutes later he carried it away – the only time I've seen any object rejected. Evidently Eve couldn't tolerate smelly trash in their home.

Although they work together, Eve and Adam specialize; he flies in the larger limbs and she never stops tinkering, rearranging the nest.

Osprey nests have toppled over from their own weight. The Brewster nest has withstood gales, floods; even small hurricanes. If humans built a nest with the same materials with their own hands, it would blow away in the next gale. But osprey utilize their beaks and talons to prune, cut, and interweave materials, and their strong wings to provide power.

Osprey share the marsh with Canada Geese, sharp-tailed saltmarsh sparrows, and several other species; the sky with crows and a variety of gulls; and the nest itself with house sparrows who love, live and raise their families in low rent tenement apartment on the sides.

Canada Goose

House Sparrows
in the nest

Saltmarsh Sparrow

Gold Finch

Willet

Red-Winged Blackbird

39

4: "For Unto Us"

A few weeks after Eve and Adam return, she lays 2 or 3 eggs over the course of a week. The eggs incubate approximately 38 days. Then around Memorial Day chicks emerge one-by-one over the same interval of time. Eve sits on the eggs whenever necessary through cold, wet spring days and nights to keep the eggs, then the chicks, warm and dry and protect them from passing predators.

40

Eve suffers far the worst of family life, often appearing bedraggled despite preening whenever possible to keep her body clean and properly oiled. Occasionally she shows modest signs of morning sickness or some other malaise: how would you like sitting 40 days on an osprey nest with two or three eggs inside you, then having to tend to the helpless young chicks that emerge from them?

In a few rare moments of overt affection
I saw Adam feeding Eve. But except for the
comparatively brief occasions when he
willingly replaces her on the nest while she
goes off to eat a fish or take a brief flight,
usually he's flying, fishing, or eating and
resting in better vented and shaded nearby
trees where he maintains a rustic,
camp-like second home.

Eve seeks relief from her lonesomeness by squawking constantly; puwe, puwe puwe; chereek, chereek, chereek or other vowel dominated calls. Ospreys have their own alphabet and calls conveying different messages. But Eve and Adam, (normally the silent type because flying around enables him to be) both know what each other is doing or saying.

It doesn't take much to ignite Eve's lonesome alarms and different calls: "Adam the photographer is back!" "Get that bird away!" "Dammit Adam, stop eating by yourself. Bring me another fish!"

Eve and Adam utilize their superlative sight and sound to recognize each other at great distance. I noted changes in Eve's behavior when Adam re-entered her world, often long before he re-entered mine.

5. Into the Wild Blue Yonder

Male osprey – all really good guys – love to fish. Their fishing dives represent one of nature's most stunning uses of highly specialized, finely tuned body parts and spectacular scenes. Their multi-faceted ability and power to fly or glide, seemingly in any direction and any speed, in many respects still exceeds that of manmade aircraft.

Osprey wings catch, push and move air with incredible power, enabling the birds to waft motionlessly or fly 1,000 miles in three days while traveling to and beyond the Caribbean for winter vacations. Their massive wings dwarf their puny flesh and bones.

An osprey's ball-like 'shoulders,' 'elbows' and 'wrists' bend in all directions, giving them contortionist ability to flex in any manner and combination, serving as parachutes, corkscrews, rudders, ailerons, giant air shovels or fins on brief underwater excursions. The wings provide exceptional strength and maneuverability, forward or straight up and down, at any speed. Osprey can lift-launch themselves straight up from land or water, or drop straight down slowly or at speed, a variety of skills no other species can match.

Long and thin but durable and strong feathers comprise over half an osprey's wing mass. Four finger-like primary feathers and a rarely seen thumb-like feather (protruding down on left wing) extend from their 'wrists' much like a human hand. Additional primary feathers line the entire outer section of their wings. Most of the feathers, including the fingers, operate under independent controls, extending in different directions to fine-tune movement.

Shoulders forward, wings, elbows and wrists, fingers and thumbs outward for control of landing.

47

Small bird. Big wings.
Note where beak protrudes from wing.

Humans learned to fly by observing and imitating osprey before making their own historic flight in 1903. Orville and Wilbur Wright traveled to Sandy Hook, New Jersey, then Cape Hatteras, North Carolina to watch and study how osprey utilized their wings to bank and maneuver. Awed by the miracles of osprey flight, the United States Marine Corps named the current tilt-rotor aircraft V-22 Osprey. These helicopters, like osprey, fly horizontally between vertical take-offs and landings.

49

50

Each osprey has literally thousands of feathers of six different varieties. Large primary feathers provide color, contour and weather protection as well as power. Smaller and lighter semi-plume and down feathers sometimes intermix with the larger feathers, sometimes lie beneath like long underwear providing effective insulation and buoyancy. Small hooks lock many feathers in place together.

Each feather operates under individual control, powered by thousands of muscles.

Moving from front to back, four different rows of feathers adorn the bottom of this osprey wings, with primary feathers on the front and back and semi-down and plume intermixed between.

Hair-like down and plume feathers cover the osprey's head and neck, sometimes blowing in the wind, clumped or individually. A mixture of primary and down feathers can be seen in the osprey's necklace/bib.

51

Osprey constantly preen
their feathers – cleaning and
relocking their minute hooks
– in their mouths.

53

Landings

Adam's other primary duty consists of patrolling the area, chasing off threats (including me if I approach too close). He soars in a regular loop, banking turns like a NASCAR racecar. In 2009 I stood up on several occasions then moved slowly closer as cautiously as possible to photograph flight, trying to position myself under Adam's loop to provide the best camera light. If I waited until just before sunset, his body would be bottom-lit.

Adam took the bait three times, gazing at me less menacingly each time. Then he realized if he flew off to his tree home, the game would be over; I was left standing with nothing to do. Eve stopped squawking too; maybe she thought I'd assumed responsibility for predator control.

6. Fishing

Fishing osprey, as noted, utilize their immense wings to soar as slowly as possible, peering intently at fish, positioning themselves as precisely as possible for a dive.

Osprey eyes offset light refraction to position a fish precisely for a dive. Adam sees a fish better from 100' above than a human eye does peering under water within a few feet.

A dark ring in each bold yellow eye and dark stripe passing over both eyes on the sides of the head enable osprey to overcome glare in the same manner as baseball players put charcoal on their cheeks.

Osprey eyes have see-through protective nictitating membranes which they pull over their eyes whenever they hit water — or an aggressive family member flaps its wings or pecks away at food or tree limbs. Sometimes osprey don't seem to have much sense concerning where the other end of a stick in their mouth or their extended wing may be, requiring nest-mates to take precaution by covering their eyes.

The underwater portion of this struggle occurs in a fish's 'home court.' If the fish is too big or too deep, an osprey loses. On rare occasions fishermen have reeled in fish with osprey skeletons attached to their backs.

But if all goes well, Adam's powerful wings lift him straight out of the water. After a brief shudder a few feet above the surface to shake water off his wings, he flies forward away from the scene of his catch.

Fish comprise 98% of osprey diets. The birds aren't particular what species they eat, although herring make fishing easiest in spring.

With talons instead of feet, osprey can't swim, paddle, or walk as well as most other maritime birds.

Adam's immense wings and tail flatten out as he strikes water to create a flat splat-like impact comparable to that of a sheet of plywood (the opposite of an alewife's blade-like body knifing up a water fall), hopefully preserving as much buoyancy as possible near the water surface. The farther Adam sinks into water, the less leverage his wings and tail have to lift him, providing modest fin-like underwater propulsion.

The lock of Adam's talons on a fish is all but irreversible; he either flies away with a dying fish or drowns. If his wings and tail remain at or near the surface he extends them up and out, grasping and pulling down air to lift himself out of the water.

Note: The photographs on pages 58 and 59 were taken in Florida.

Shaking the water off.

Adam frequently makes a low pass over the nest to show off his catch, then retreats across the creek to the camp he maintains in the woods to eat the front half of the fish bite-by-bite. He dines in full view of Eve, whose squawking intensifies until he is done. When he finishes his meal he returns with the rear end of the fish to the nest, where he solidly anchors the remainder with one foot. In peak fishing season, osprey rarely leave a piece of anchored fish on the nest.

Adam briefly stands proudly over the fish, lording over Eve, until she runs out of patience, wrests the fish away with little resistance, then flies up on the video camera for a short dinner break.

Evidently well fed on this rainy day, Adam returns to the nest with an entire alewife for Eve.

Adam stomping on fish.

Eve grasping fish.

61

Eve enjoys dinner as intestine flies off into space.

Scup this evening!

64

Ugh! It's a carp!

65

7. More Mouths to Feed

If April is a month for osprey to form family relationships and rebuild a nest, and May to sit on eggs; June and July are months for young osprey to transform themselves to fully grown birds.

Osprey chicks enter the world, helpless and blind, about the size of a plum, clad in fuzzy light brown down, with disproportionately top-heavy large heads and necks.

Chicks grow very rapidly. Young osprey gain 80% of weight in the first 30 days of their life by rapidly converting fish into body parts. The chick's day-to-day change becomes noticeable, with the size difference between the first and last born increasing briefly then all but disappearing in Eve and Adam's comparatively well fed home.

The mother feeds her young, which quickly learn to wobble up for food. She also keeps them warm and dry. Eve will stand over her chicks in heavy rain, burrowing both wings into the nest's soft floor, transforming her body into an igloo-shaped structure to make sure no water reach them.

Life on the nest becomes far more frantic after the chicks arrive: more mouths to feed, more children to protect and keep out of harm's way, more fish to catch, and more work keeping house. Protective ramparts rise steadily, sometimes frantically transferred from side-to-side to protect against threatening winds. The nest becomes ever more crowded although Adam spends increasingly more time away.

Young osprey begin flapping their disproportionately large wings and hopping around, ducking each other's moves. Eve becomes a master at that.

Every act of osprey life has a purpose. In 2009 the three young osprey often formed an orderly food line, in which the oldest (a female) in the front always seemed to get more fish than the youngest at the end.

In 2010, the oldest (a male) always stood front-left with his foot anchoring the fish. While the middle juvenile watched benignly, the bird on the right squawked constantly lest it might not get enough or any at all, constantly looking for an opportunity to sneak over and grasp the fish often precipitating a tug-of-war. The dominant juvenile always let the youngest eat a little.

In 2009, a relatively slow fishing year, strife evolved at the nest from 'foreign' osprey flying over looking for unanchored fish. True to nature, Eve adopted as large and menacing a countenance as possible, and hid fish beneath her wings, hoping to intimidate potential attackers.

8. Flight training

As juvenile osprey reach full size, they constantly stretch their wings, crowding the nest. Adam is rarely seen there except when bringing home fish.

Despite their relatively equal size, the gap because the first and last born osprey increases learning to fly and fish, perhaps because differences in their psyches linger longer than those of their bodies. The oldest juvenile quickly begins flapping its wings and jumping about to gauge the power of flight.

Adam ducking
Eve's wing

76

First flight

Crowded nest

The juveniles frequently become airborne, flying above the nest before they dare fly away.

The youngest osprey delays taking risks, particularly jumping off the nest for its first flight. In 2010 I watched it squawk for an hour after its first flight after flying over to the trees surrounding Adam's other home, where unfamiliar branches obstructed its wings as it maneuvered to gather the nerve to jump off for the return flight.

Adam watched calmly from a limb above.

After juvenile
osprey learn to feed
themselves with fish Adam
brings, Eve quickly heads south, leaving
the teenagers home alone for a month or more.
Tired of the nest, she heads back as far south as
the Amazon, for business and pleasure of her own.

In 2009 after Eve departed, a 'foreign' osprey attacked
the nest, ending up standing atop the senior juvenile who
lay flat on her back with their talons entwined. Lying on
the back is osprey posture for fending off an attack. The
two bounced up quickly then stood side-by-side eyeing
each other. Then the original occupant and her siblings
flew away after which the attacker hopped up temporarily
to take command of the roost.

The next day life on the nest seemed normal.

As the two combatants disengaged, blood was visible on both where their talons had become intertwined.

86

9. Evolution

The two young osprey that occupied the Brewster nest in 2011 behaved very differently from their predecessors, with the female acting far more liberated.

On my first visit I witnessed a love triangle as a male osprey waltzed and sang high o'er the female on the nest, wooing her to fly away with him. Ignored, he landed beside, standing nervously: wings spread for quick departure. Another male swooped down almost immediately and all three flew away.

One male flew up the creek with the female. Then a lone male returned to the nest, standing proudly like king of the realm.

I'm not sure whether that escapade changed the pair on the nest. The next day two began building enthusiastically together. But both osprey constantly crouched, ready to fly, rather than proudly posing side-by-side as in previous years.

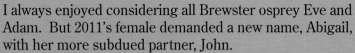

I always enjoyed considering all Brewster osprey Eve and Adam. But 2011's female demanded a new name, Abigail, with her more subdued partner, John.

Abigail didn't want to settle down and fuss about tidying the nest.

John assumed an unusual urgency bringing sticks.

For several weeks the nest resembled a camp site as much as a home.

John's seductive moves grew more urgent, even desperate.

Abigail didn't appear to enjoy sex; John became even more obsessed. One morning he leapt on her head as the sun rose, silhouetting their posture. She rarely responded, leaving him facing every which way on her back. Once she picked up a mouthful of grass as he maneuvered unsuccessfully atop.

Abigail laid three eggs a week later than usual, spread out over a few more days. Still the modern woman, initially she didn't sit on the eggs, more prone than her elders to abandon the nest, making me wonder whether the eggs were warm enough, and forcing the more responsible John to sit.

For several weeks Abigail and John both acted more like the opposite sex. John sat while Abigail stood and flew over him.

As the nest reached new heights, Abigail, a tomboy, frolicked around, while John, roles reversed, squawked on the nest pleading for her return.

When Abigail failed to respond, John, without changing expression, launched himself to take off in pursuit. Note his upside down wing, seemingly poised to flip over and to increase takeoff power.

92

Once Abigail headed across the creek to the trees where Adam had maintained his second home in prior years. Frequently she vacated the nest for considerable periods of time, far longer than females in prior years.

But eventually Abigail began to nudge John to leave, then replace him on the eggs after standing briefly over him. The two osprey, at John's lead, settled into equal alternating time shifts; as one returned the other departed with little communication other than a nudge.

Abigail's first chick arrived in early June, a week later than usual. She converted to more normal female behavior two days before, as if hormones told her babies were coming.

The third egg – probably the first laid – never hatched; I assume lost to cold.

John began to do all the fishing, while Abigail remained on the nest squawking normally for more food, particularly when days warmed and fishing slowed.

As summer progressed Abigail, although forever restless to do a little flying and fishing herself, became an exemplary mother, making the nest into a never-ending theater of scenes I'd never seen before.

During a severe daylong heat wave Abigail made herself into a tent to shield her juveniles, as all three panted with mouths wide open and tongues hanging out.

Partly to compensate for her own wanderlust, Abigail imposed higher standards of nest discipline on her juveniles, particularly to stay out of sight whenever necessary. But, as with all teenagers, discipline diminished as the juveniles grew.

Abigail never lost her multi-task sense of wanderlust, seizing every opportunity to fly short patrols in John's absence, take a quick spin along the creek for sticks or fish or to control events from nearby trees, while always remaining in sight of the nest.

Frequently she waltzed through every possible position while landing, as if rehearsing or just having fun.

Abigail cruising the adjacent creek in view of the nest, hoping to get lucky and catch her own fish.

One afternoon after a particularly slow fishing day, Abigail and John enjoyed a prolonged sand shark dinner together while their hungry offspring watched.

A few days later, when John returned with another fish, instead of grabbing it to feed herself and/or the juveniles, Abigail watched as John fed them, showing more overt preference for one than Abigail or any mother ever did.

10. Forever After

Do adult osprey ever see and recognize their offspring and siblings again?

Other than the small handful of birds tagged by Rob Bierregaard, after Eve, Adam, Abigail, John or other osprey fly south no one knows where they go, what they do, or how and when they die. Most osprey return to Cape Cod, in the same unrecorded bird anonymity from which they left. Indeed, if some future summer an adult osprey neighbors with one of its many young, no one knows for sure if they recognize each other. With such acute powers of sound and sight, they certainly might; returning mates find their way thousands of miles back to their nest and seemingly recognize each other. But, just as sibling osprey sometimes fight or even kill each other over fish, it's doubtful family recognition changes survival behavior on nature's food chain.

Migrating osprey don't carry passports or recognize international boundaries.

Bierregaard has placed electronic transmitters on osprey since 2000 to map their southern winter migrations. He found that juvenile osprey act like teenage kids after they leave parental supervision, which sometimes becomes fatal given the journeys they must take.

In 2008 'Meadow', a young male left Martha's Vineyard in August – headed north, not south. 'Meadow' approached Hudson Bay before becoming cold, at which time he traveled 1,500 miles west to Lake Superior, before getting cold again. Finally he flew out of the country to the Dominican Republic, where he got shot at a fish farm. Osprey don't carry guns; they defend themselves with their own wits and bodies, which particularly in youth sometimes fail them in deciding where and when to travel.

'Belle', a juvenile female, left Martha's Vineyard in October 2010 headed south, after a short junket up to southern New Hampshire. Bierregaard believes a 50 MPH wind that closed the local airport may have blown Belle off island after a day at the beach. She passed within 200 miles of Bermuda, much further out to sea than osprey normally travel, then veered westward two days before landing in Haiti. Eventually she traveled further into Brazil than any other recorded osprey.

In November, 2010, 'Thatch", another juvenile, flew into Tropical Storm Tomas south of Cuba. Although I watched a juvenile clinging to the Brewster nest for eight hours during Tropical Storm Irene in 2011, then fly slowly off into the wind, osprey sometimes have little choice but to blow with the wind: the storm carried Thatch several hundred miles west. After the storm he headed south again, before veering back to the east, then south again. All told he traveled three sides of a rectangle in 66 hours, 1,100 miles, to resume his original track.

Since the ice age created Cape Cod, adventuresome, four-month old, four pound osprey have flown without baggage or food to South America for winter vacation. Juveniles normally fly three days never before having been where they are going, but making logical course changes to get there. None has been known to fly too far out into the Atlantic and die.

In contrast in 1620 the Pilgrims took 62 days crossing the Atlantic, intending to land at the mouth of the Hudson River in New York, but disembarking in Provincetown, MA instead. Charles Lindbergh didn't make the first manned flight across the Atlantic until 1927.

What about bird brains make them so far superior to humans at so few limited tasks? Humans definitely aren't the smartest at everything.

Juvenile osprey get attacked and killed by owls in the New England woods, land on the Dominican Republic or Cuba – not wise choices for osprey to visit – and make other fatal mistakes. Bierregaard and other naturalists believe many die on their first winter migration, but far fewer as mature adults afterward. Adults, which learn after their first migration to stick to the eastern coastline coming and going, often survive into their twenties.

Young male osprey return to the area of their birth at age 3 as male rivals seeking a nest, not loving sons. Young female osprey exhibit less place loyalty seeking a mate and nest, perhaps to minimize inbreeding.

As summer ends the three juvenile osprey leave the nest, one-by-one, several weeks apart.

These two, however, are Abigail's offspring, one with a far larger and floppier necklace/bib than her mother's.

The youngest osprey, abandoned by its siblings, enjoyed having the nest to itself after their departure for several weeks, and Adam seemed to enjoy the less stressful one-on-one relationship.

107

Whenever I watch osprey
I can't help but ponder the contrast
between their unchanging life and the increasing destruction
of resources (including other species) spinning from man's
ever-growing materialism. Recently I saw a chart reporting
the declining number of large animal species living in the wild,
only 3,200 tigers and 600,000 African elephants, compared to
a steadily increasing 7,000,000,000 human beings. Without
significant change in human behavior, all wild animals may
be gone before too many more years, along with the largest
birds and fish.

I'd rather fly like an osprey for a day than be President of Bank
America, or ride into space on a NASA rocket. Big banking
has become imprisoned in the false values of today's America,
while NASA provides a programmed cage-like ride. Think of
the joy and freedom commuting to work high over woods and
water instead of down congested roads; going fishing wherever
and whenever I choose. And think about seven months of
winter vacation on the Amazon or some romantic island
without hassling with airlines, after five summer months of
renewed courtship, child rearing, and fishing on Cape Cod.

Seems like paradise to me.

October 26, 2011

AUTHORS NOTE

I came to Cape Cod in 1982 somewhat by chance, having studied then worked in Boston the previous 18 years. When I decided to move I sought a banking job "anywhere in Massachusetts or the three northern New England states except Boston", which I guess says something about me. Cape Cod provided the first opening. Prior to that my outdoor views all arose in the New Hampshire woods where I grew up.

Cape Cod's environmental uniqueness grows on you. For example, it didn't take long to realize I passed through three different weather patterns evolving from three very different bodies of water on my regular 25 mile bike training route out of Brewster. It took a few more years to learn that the water flowing in and out of Lower Mill Pond right behind my home passed through five different ecosystems in 3 and ½ miles, with two of Wayne Peterson's Massachusetts Important Bird Areas on each end. Indeed, an economics major, I don't recall when I learned the definition of "ecosystem".

Along the way my community banking job provided me the opportunity to work with and make good friends with the people at many Cape Cod environmental organizations including:

The Friends of the Cape Cod National Seashore

The Center for Coastal Studies in Provincetown

The Cape Cod Museum of Natural History in Brewster

Massachusetts Audubon's sanctuaries in Wellfleet and Barnstable

The International Fund for Animal Welfare (IFAW) in Yarmouth

The Brewster Conservation Trust and the Compact of Cape Cod Cons. Trusts

The Association for the Preservation of Cape Cod

Cape Cod Commercial Hook Fisherman's Association

All played a role in inducing me to worry considerably more about the planet my grandson will live in 50 years from now than how many homes are built on Cape Cod to support the economy this year.

I was neither a birder nor a photographer in 2005 when I retired from my executive banking responsibilities. Indeed I wouldn't label myself either today. But about that time new cameras facilitated photographing birds in ways never possible before. I became hooked, soon realizing the best place to photograph birds is at their nests, including the osprey nest on the marsh about a mile from my home – as peaceful a place as I know to sit and contemplate the view.

Many people assisted me completing this book:

Jill Maraghy, who took my photographs and words and compiled them into a work of art,

Seth Rolbein, who proofread the book,

Wayne Peterson, who wrote the forward, and Seth, Peter Trull and Fred O'Regan who so eloquently endorsed it,

Joe Mault at Orleans Camera who has always helped me make my pictures look better,

the people at Paraclete Press who printed this book,

my wife Sue, who reviewed the same pictures and words over and over again, (More diversified than I, she also photographs plants and other more mundane objects, including people,)

and hundreds of other friends, who stimulated my growing addiction to Cape Cod's unique natural features and beauty.

MY THANKS TO ALL OF YOU

Elliott Carr